Mieke Sprenger

# Parchment Craft, my life

# Colofon

Pergamano® is the brand under which books
and materials especially for Parchment Craft
are brought onto the market.

For information:

Pergamano International
P.O. box 86
1420 AB Uithoorn
The Netherlands
Tel: +31 (0)297 522533
Fax: +31 (0)297 526256
E-mail: info@pergamano.com
Website: www.pergamano.com

©2006, Pergamano International, Uithoorn, The Netherlands

ISBN 9077173498
NUR 475

Author: Mieke Sprenger, Vinkeveen
Design: Mieke Sprenger, Vinkeveen
Photography: Ferry Herrebrugh, Amstelveen, The Netherlands
Layout and typesetting: Helfensteijn de Vreugd, Uithoorn, The Netherlands
Printing: Hoonte Bosch & Keuning, Utrecht, The Netherlands

# Contents

# Foreword

You are holding the first book by Mieke Sprenger and I am honoured to write a preface in this book on behalf of the publisher. I have known Mieke for almost 20 years now; she was one of the first enthusiastic ladies in the Netherlands, who embraced parchment craft from the very beginning.

I met Mieke at the People's University in Amstelveen (The Netherlands), where I taught Pergamano® classes. I soon noticed that Mieke had the ambition to become a teacher herself. That would allow her to teach classes and actively be involved with the hobby. Over the years, Mieke has developed into a true jack-of-all-trades. She is very creative and has designed many patterns. In addition, there is a good chance that you will run into her at a demonstration or at hobby fairs.

She is always prepared to help others. The way she does this sometimes makes me wonder if she has more hours in a day than I do! I have regularly asked her to help me with the preparations of the Pergamano® books that I have made n the past. Our collaboration has always been pleasant thanks to her positive attitude and the fact that we are both passionate about our hobby.

I think it is fantastic that Mieke has now made her own pattern book so that she can present her ideas and inspire readers to practice this multi-faceted hobby. Her contribution is very welcome; as the hobby grows, so does the demand for a variety of pattern books.

Mieke, I would like to take this opportunity to thank you again for your constant dedication. You have helped to maintain and distribute our hobby. So, I offer you a warm welcome as a Pergamano® author, congratulations on your book and the best of luck!

Dear reader, if you are already an enthusiast, then you already know that parchment craft is a fascinating and multi-faceted hobby that continues to provide new challenges. I am convinced that Mieke's book will be a new source of inspiration and I wish you many creative hours working from it.
If you are new to the hobby then I would like to say the following. Give it a try; the hobby sometimes looks difficult, but you can make it as easy as you yourself like. There are also easy ways to start the hobby without excessive costs. I wish you lots of luck*!

Kind regards,

Martha Ospina
Author and President of The International Parchment Craft Academy

*For detailed information about the hobby and the many possibilities, visit www.pergamano.com.*

# Introduction

My name will sound familiar to many of you. I have been active as a teacher for many years, regularly emonstrate at hobby fairs and for 12,5 years, I have been an editor of the definitive magazine for parchment craft: 'Pergamano World'.

It was back in 1989 that I first came in contact with Pergamano® through a friend. I was immediately impressed and subsequently enrolled for a class at the people's university in Amstelveen (The Netherlands). At the time, the class was given by Martha Ospina herself. After this introductory class, I was so enthusiastic that I started training as a Pergamano® teacher. After I became a teacher, I taught for five years at the people's university in Geleen (The Netherlands).

During that period, I kept in touch with Martha and started focusing more and more on designing patterns and storing them on the computer. In this way, I worked behind the scenes on a number of publications. In the end, I took the plunge and made my own book, which I am now proud to present to you.

In this beautiful book, you will find a large number of pieces. Naturally, you can create them according to the instructions, but try using your own inspiration as well. You will be amazed by the possibilities and the results.

For many years, parchment craft has been gaining popularity in an increasing number of countries. This is thanks in particular to Martha Ospina, who has put the hobby on the map, all over the world. I am very grateful to her, because I have learned so much from her over the years. Even so much, that my hobby is now my work.

I took great pleasure in designing the projects in this book for you. I could not have done it without the support of my friends and my husband. I would like to offer them my heartfelt thanks. I hope that you have as much pleasure making the projects and I wish you lots of luck.

Mieke Sprenger

# General materials, abbreviations, explanations of techniques, tips

Here is a list of the general materials you will need for the pieces in this book. In addition, each description lists the additional materials needed for that specific piece. A number is listed between parentheses after all Pergamano® materials; this is the product code.

## You will need
- mapping tool (1420)
- brush no. 2, Kolinsky (1425)
- tear-off palette (1806)
- embossing/perforating pad excellent (1419)
- embossing pad de luxe (1413)
- pointed scissors stainless steel (1132) or
- perga cutter (1135)
- perga spray (1808)
- perga glue (1805)
- perga kit (1411)
- if desired, fan sponge (1429)
- cutting mat or sheet of cardboard to work on
- removable tape
- white pencil
- if desired, ruler
- glass of water
- paper tissues
- regular scissors

## Abbreviations in description
| | |
|---|---|
| **T** | = tinta, |
| **T pearl** | = tinta pearl |
| **T pastel** | = tinta pastel |
| **P** | = pintura |
| **P perla** | = pinta perla |
| **PCE** | = perga colors exclusive |

## Explanation of techniques

### PAINTING 1
If the painted colours are applied one layer at a time (Dresden flower technique, perga liner or perga color technique), then the colours are separated by a comma.

### PAINTING 2
If multiple colours are picked up on the brush, it is indicated with a +; in this case, the colours mix while you are painting.

### PAINTING 3
If the colours are mixed in advance on the tear-off palette, it is indicated in the instructions with the word "mixed."

### DORSING
Dorsing is in principle done on the back of the piece. If you are supposed to dorse on the front, it will be clearly specified in the instructions.

### EMBOSSING
See comment above under dorsing.

# Bordeaux set: bookmark

The following are general instructions for the bookmark, square card and box.
If a certain piece of text is specifically for one of the three objects, then this is indicated.

## BOOKMARK, GENERAL
The bookmark is made of fantasy parchment bordeaux.
The extra front sheet is made of ordinary parchment paper.
3-D elements: 4x flowers made of fantasy parchment bordeaux.

## CARD, GENERAL
The card is made of fantasy parchment bordeaux. The extra
front sheet is made of ordinary parchment paper. 3-D elements:
1x flower made of fantasy parchment bordeaux.

## BOX, GENERAL
The box is made of fantasy parchment bordeaux and the lid
is made of ordinary parchment paper. 3-D elements:
1x flower made of fantasy parchment bordeaux.

## TRACING
1 white: entire pattern.

## PERFORATING (SHALLOW)
With perforating tool 4-needle: according to pattern.

## EMBOSSING
With embossing tool small ball: dots between 4-needle
erforations. With embossing tool extra fine ball: hearts,
flower designs and decorative lines.

## PERFORATING (DEEP)
With perforating tool 4-needle: a second time according
to pattern.

# Bordeaux set: card & box

## CUTTING
Cut 4-needle perforations into crosses and slots.

## FINISHING BOOKMARK
Cut the fantasy parchment bordeaux to size. Cut the extra front sheet out along the 4-needle perforations. Attach it to the fantasy parchment bordeaux with perga glue. Cut the 3-D flowers out, emboss them and attach them to the extra front sheet with dabs of perga kit. Attach the beads in the flower hearts with perga glue.

## FINISHING CARD
Fold the card. Perforate with the 4-needle tool along the card outline (through 2 layers). Cut the card out along these perforations. Cut the extra front sheet out along the 4-needle perforations. Attach it to the fantasy parchment bordeaux with perga glue. Cut the 3-D flower out, emboss it and attach it to the extra front sheet with dabs of perga kit. Attach the bead in the flower heart with perga glue.

## FINISHING BOX
Emboss the fold lines with embossing tool fine stylus. Cut the box and the lid out along the outline. Cut three strips - 11 cm long and 3mm wide - from the fantasy parchment bordeaux. Thread them through the 4-needle perforations that have been cut into slots in the lid. Cut a piece of fantasy parchment to size and attach it behind the top of the lid with perga glue. Attach the sticking strips of the box together with double-sided tape. Cut the 3-D flower out, emboss it and attach it to the extra front sheet with dabs of perga kit. Attach the bead in the flower heart with perga glue.

# Orange flower set: large card

*The following are general instructions for this set of three cards. If a certain piece of text is specifically for one of the three cards, then this is indicated.*

### GENERAL
The outer card is made of ordinary parchment paper. The inner card is made of fantasy parchment apricot orange. For the 7-cornered card and small rectangular card, you will also need: orange/brown ribbon 2x ±40cm (Ø 3mm).

### TRACING
White pencil: fold line. T black: entire pattern.

### PAINTING WITH PERGA COLORS EXCLUSIVE
On the back: PCE16: leaves. PCE3: flower(s). PCE3 and PCE19 mixed: flower heart(s).

### COLORING WITH PERGA COLORS EXCLUSIVE
On front: PCE16: between black lines along card outline.

### PERFORATING (SHALLOW)
With perforating tool 4-needle: according to pattern.

### EMBOSSING
With embossing tool fine stylus: fold line. With embossing tool small ball: dots and lines between 4-needle perforations, leaves (lightly). With embossing tool large ball: flower(s) and flower heart(s).

### PERFORATING (DEEP)
With perforating tool 4-needle: a second time according to pattern.

### CUTTING
Cut 4-needle perforations into crosses and slots.

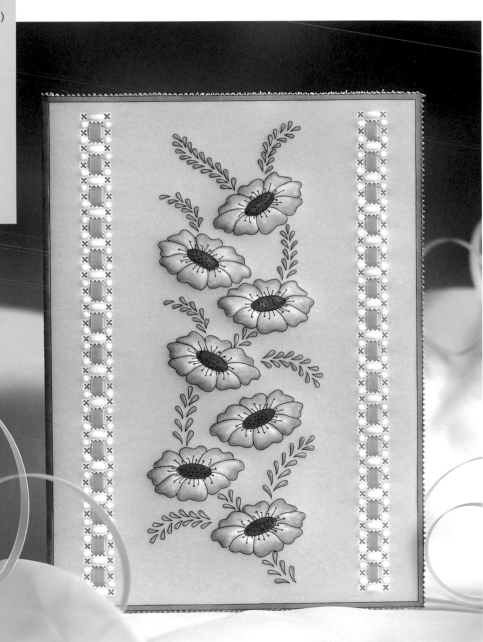

# Orange flower set:
## 7-cornered & small rectangular card

### FINISHING LARGE CARD

Cut two strips – 13.5 cm long and 3mm wide - from the fantasy parchment apricot orange. Thread them through the 4-needle perforations that have been cut into slots. Attach an oversized extra inner card made of fantasy parchment apricot orange inside the outer card with removable tape. Perforate with perforating tool 2-needle along the card outline (through 4 layers). Cut the inner card and outer card out along these perforations. Attach the inner card in the card with double-sided tape.

### FINISHING 7-CORNERED CARD AND SMALL RECTANGULAR CARD

Attach an oversized extra inner card made of fantasy parchment apricot orange inside the outer card with removable tape. Perforate with perforating tool 2-needle along the card outline (through 4 layers). Cut the inner card and outer card out along these perforations. Attach the inner card in the card with double-sided tape. Attach the orange/brown ribbon at the fold line and tie it in a knot.

## YOU WILL NEED

parchment paper:
parchment paper (1406)
fantasy parchment
bordeaux (1588)

tinta:
gold (1210)
white (1201)

perforating tools:
1-needle (11041)
2-needle (11061)

embossing tools:
fine stylus (11031)
small ball (11011)
star (1122)

white beads (21x)

pattern: page 36

# Flower beads

### GENERAL
The outer card is made of ordinary parchment paper; the inner card is made of fantasy parchment bordeaux. 3-D elements: 21x flowers of ordinary parchment paper.

### TRACING
White pencil: fold line. T gold: card outline, wisps on flowers, flower hearts of three large flowers. T white: outline of three large flowers.

### EMBOSSING
With embossing tool fine stylus: fold line. With embossing tool small ball: wisps on flowers, card outline. With embossing tool star: according to pattern.

### STIPPLING
With 1-needle tool: three large flowers.

### FINISHING
Fold the outer card. Perforate with perforating tool 2-needle along the card outline (through 2 layers). Cut the card out along these perforations. Cut the inner card to size and attach it inside the card with double-sided tape. Cut the 3-D flowers out, emboss them and attach them to the front sheet of the outer card with dabs of perga kit. Attach the beads in the 3-D flowers with perga glue.

## YOU WILL NEED

parchment paper:
parchment paper (1406)
fantasy parchment
bordeaux (1588

tinta:
gold (1210)
white (1201)

perforating tools:
2-needle (11061)

embossing tools:
fine stylus (11031)
small ball (11011)

pattern: page 38

### GENERAL

The outer card is made of ordinary parchment paper; the inner card is made of fantasy parchment bordeaux.

### TRACING

White pencil: fold line. T gold: card outline, dots and ornaments. T white: flowers and leaves.

### PERFORATING (SHALLOW)

With perforating tool 2-needle: between ornaments.

### EMBOSSING

With embossing tool fine stylus: fold line. With embossing tool small ball: flowers, leaves (lightly), between lines of ornaments.

### PERFORATING (DEEP)

With perforating tool 2-needle: a second time between ornaments.

### CUTTING

Cut 2-needle perforations out between ornaments.

### FINISHING

Fold the card and perforate with perforating tool 2-needle along the card outline (through 2 layers). Cut the card out along these perforations. Cut the inner card to size and attach it inside the card with double-sided tape.

# Floral fantasy in turquoise

## YOU WILL NEED

parchment paper:
parchment paper (1406)
fantasy parchment
ice blue (1590)

tinta:
black (1202)

perforating tools:
2-needle (11061)
five in circle (1123)

embossing tools:
fine stylus (11031)
small ball (11011)
extra large ball (1099)

perga colors exclusive (1431)

pattern: page 36

### GENERAL

The outer card is made of ordinary parchment paper and the inner card is made of fantasy parchment ice blue.

### TRACING

White pencil: fold line. T black: entire pattern.

### PAINTING WITH PERGA COLORS EXCLUSIVE

PCE13: four flowers on the left. PCE14: three small flowers, outer edge of three fantasy flowers on the left. PCE12: inner edge of three fantasy flowers on the left. PCE2: flower heart of four flowers on the left, three small flowers. PCE17: leaves. PCE15: veins in leaves.

### COLORING WITH PERGA COLORS EXCLUSIVE

On front: PCE14: edge in card outline, border of central circle, four 'hooks' beside central circle, PCE12: flower hearts of three fantasy flowers on the right.

### PERFORATING (SHALLOW)

With perforating tool five in circle: according to pattern.

### EMBOSSING

With embossing tool fine stylus: fold line. With embossing tool small ball: circles between five in circle perforations, smaller flowers. With embossing tool extra large ball: large flowers.

### PERFORATING (DEEP)

With perforating tool five in circle: a second time according to pattern. With perforating tool 2-needle: along inside of central border according to pattern.

### CUTTING

Cut central border out along the inner 2-needle perforations.

### FINISHING

Attach an oversized extra inner card made of fantasy parchment ice blue inside the outer card with removable tape. Perforate with perforating tool 2-needle along the card outline (through 4 layers). Cut the inner card and outer card out along these perforations. Attach the inner card in the card with double-sided tape.

# Elegant card with 3-D flowers

### GENERAL
The card is made of ordinary parchment paper and the insert sheet is made of parchment paper rainbow pastel. 3-D elements: 16x leaves, made of parchment paper rainbow pastel, 8x small flowers and 3x large flowers, both made of ordinary parchment paper.

### TRACING
White pencil: fold line. T white: 3-D elements. T gold: entire pattern.

### PERFORATING
With perforating tool 2-needle: along the inside of the central border.

### PERFORATING WITH EASY GRID
With perforating tool arrow on easy grid fine mesh: according to pattern A.

### EMBOSSING
With embossing tool fine stylus: fold line. With embossing tool small ball: dots between easy grid perforations. With embossing tool large ball: between ornaments.

### CUTTING
Cut central border out along the inner 2-needle perforations.

### FINISHING
Attach an oversized extra inner card made of fantasy parchment rainbow pastel inside the card with removable tape. Perforate with perforating tool 2-needle along the card outline (through 3 layers). Cut the card and the insert sheet out along these perforations. Attach the insert sheet in the card with double-sided tape. Emboss the 3-D elements with embossing tool small ball, cut them out and attach them to the front sheet of the card with dabs of perga kit (see colour example).

## YOU WILL NEED

parchment paper:
parchment paper (1406)
fantasy parchment
salmon pink (1589)

tinta:
gold (1210)
leaf green (1213)
pastel pink (1233)

pintura:
yellow ochre (1312)

perforating tools:
2-needle (11061)
arrow (1124)

easy grid:
fine mesh (1461)

embossing tools:
fine stylus (11031)
extra fine ball (11071)
small ball (11011)
large ball (11021)

perga colors exclusive (1431)

pattern: page 37

# Heart card

### GENERAL

The outer card is made of ordinary parchment paper and the inner card is made of fantasy parchment salmon pink. An insert sheet made of ordinary white paper is attached inside the inner card.

### TRACING

White pencil: fold line. T gold: ornaments.
T leaf green: leaves. T pastel pink: flowers.

### PAINTING

T leaf green: leaves. T pastel pink + PCE4: flowers.
P yellow ochre: flower hearts.

### PERFORATING

With perforating tool 2-needle: between ornaments.

### PERFORATING WITH EASY GRID

With perforating tool arrow on easy grid fine mesh;
according to pattern A.

### EMBOSSING

With embossing tool fine stylus: fold line. With embossing tool extra fine ball: lines between easy grid perforations. With embossing tool small ball: flower hearts. With embossing tool large ball: flowers and ornaments.

### CUTTING

Cut 2-needle perforations out between ornaments. Cut easy grid perforations into crosses, see colour example.

### FINISHING

Attach an oversized extra inner card made of fantasy parchment salmon pink inside the outer card with removable tape. Perforate with perforating tool 2-needle along the card outline (through 4 layers). Cut the inner card and outer card out along these perforations. Attach the inner card in the outer card with double-sided tape. Cut the insert sheet to size and attach it inside the inner card using double-sided tape.

## YOU WILL NEED

parchment paper:
parchment paper (1406)
fantasy parchment
ice blue (1590)

tinta:
gold (1210)
white (1201)

perforating tools:
2-needle (11061)
4-needle (11051)

embossing tools:
fine stylus (11031)
small ball (11011)
large ball (11021)

perga colors
exclusive (1431))

pattern: page 44

### GENERAL
The outer card is made of ordinary parchment paper and the inner card is made of fantasy parchment ice blue. An insert sheet made of ordinary white paper is attached inside the inner card.

### TRACING
White pencil: fold line. T gold: ornaments, small arcs in edge, flower hearts, veins in leaves. T white: large arcs in edge, flowers and leaves.

### PAINTING WITH PERGA COLORS EXCLUSIVE
PCE14: ornaments, small arcs in edge, flower hearts.

### PERFORATING (SHALLOW)
With perforating tool 4-needle: according to pattern.
With perforating tool 2-needle: according to pattern.

### EMBOSSING
With embossing tool fine stylus: fold line.
With embossing tool small ball: circles between 4-needle perforations, large arcs in edge. With embossing tool large ball: ornaments and flowers.

### PERFORATING (DEEP)
With perforating tools 2-needle and 4-needle: a second time according to pattern.

### CUTTING
Cut 4-needle perforations into crosses. Cut 2-needle perforations out between small and large arcs in edge.

### FINISHING
Attach an oversized extra inner card made of fantasy parchment ice blue inside the outer card with removable tape. Perforate with perforating tool 2-needle along the card outline (through 4 layers). Cut the inner card and outer card out along these perforations. Attach the inner card in the outer card with double-sided tape. Cut the insert sheet to size and attach it inside the inner card using double-sided tape.

## GENERAL

The outer card is made of ordinary parchment paper and the inner card is made of fantasy parchment hydrangea purple.

## TRACING

White pencil: fold line. T gold: circles between 4-needle perforations, curly line at each flower.

## PAINTING

T pastel pink + PCE9: ornaments in card outline, flowers. T pastel green + PCE17: leaves. T gold: flower hearts.

## PERFORATING (SHALLOW)

With perforating tool 4-needle: according to pattern.

## EMBOSSING

With embossing tool fine stylus: fold line. With embossing tool small ball: dots between 4-needle perforations, ornaments in card outline, flowers and leaves (lightly).

## PERFORATING (DEEP)

With perforating tool 4-needle: a second time according to pattern.

## CUTTING

Cut 4-needle perforations into crosses and slots.

## FINISHING

With T gold: fine lines on petals. Attach an oversized extra inner card made of fantasy parchment hydrangea purple inside the outer card with removable tape. Perforate with perforating tool 2-needle along the card outline (through 4 layers).
Cut the inner card and outer card out along these perforations. Attach the inner card in the outer card with double-sided tape.

## YOU WILL NEED

parchment paper:
parchment paper (1406)

tinta:
white (1201)
gold (1210)

dorso nature colors (1444)
colour light green

dorso bright colours (1443)
colour pink

perforating tools:
4-needle (11051)

embossing tools:
fine stylus (11031)
small ball (11011)
large ball (11021)

perga liners
combi box (1452)

pattern: page 42

# Ornament card

### GENERAL
The outer card and the inner card are made of ordinary parchment paper. The insert sheet is made of ordinary white paper.

### TRACING
White pencil: fold line.
T white: card outline.
T gold: ornaments.

### DORSING WITH DORSO OIL
With dorso light green: on front sheet of inner card along card outline. With dorso pink: on front sheet of inner card behind flower design.

### PAINTING WITH PERGA LINERS
B1, B5, A1, A6: flowers. B8, A20, A19, A17: flower hearts. B8, B7, A15, A14: small leaves. B8, B6, A15, A14: large leaves.

### PERFORATING (SHALLOW)
With perforating tool 4-needle: according to pattern.

### EMBOSSING
With embossing tool fine stylus: fold line. With embossing tool small ball: ornaments, dots between 4-needle perforations. With embossing tool large ball: flowers and leaves.

### PERFORATING (DEEP)
With perforating tool 4-needle: a second time according to pattern.

### CUTTING
Cut 4-needle perforations into crosses.

### FINISHING
Fold the card. Perforate with the 4-needle tool along the card outline and cut the card out along these perforations. Cut the inner card and the insert sheet to size. Attach the inner card in the outer card with double-sided tape. Attach the insert sheet in the inner card with double-sided tape.

## YOU WILL NEED

parchment paper:
parchment paper (1406)
fantasy parchment
red (1598)

tinta:
gold (1210)
leaf green (1213)

perforating tools:
2-needle (11061)
arrow (1124)

easy grid:
fine mesh (1461)

embossing tools:
fine stylus (11031)
small ball (11011)
large ball (11021)

perga liners
combi box (1452)

pattern: page 37

# Christmas rose in star

### GENERAL
The outer card is made of ordinary parchment paper and the inner card is made of fantasy parchment red.

### TRACING
White pencil: fold line. T gold: outline of stars. T leaf green: leaves.

### PAINTING WITH PERGA LINERS
B1, A1, A12: flowers. A17, A19: flower hearts. B8, B15, A16, A19: large leaves at bottom of flowers. B7, A15: small leaves. B15, A16, A3, A17, A1: pine branches. B11, A12: piece of ribbon at bottom of flower bouquet, berries. A1: shiny spots on berries. A3: black dot on berries.

### PERFORATING WITH EASY GRID
With perforating tool arrow on easy grid fine mesh: according to pattern A on part A.

### EMBOSSING
With embossing tool fine stylus: fold line. With embossing tool small ball: dots between easy grid perforations, between outlines of small star, pine branches and leaves. With embossing tool large ball: between outlines of large star, on front: flowers.

### CUTTING
Cut easy grid perforations out according to cutting pattern.

### FINISHING
Attach an oversized extra inner card made of fantasy parchment red inside the outer card with removable tape. Perforate with perforating tool 2-needle along the card outline (through 4 layers). Cut the inner card and outer card out along these perforations. Attach the inner card in the outer card with double-sided tape.

parchment paper:
parchment paper (1406)
fantasy parchment
ice blue (1590)

tinta:
gold (1210)
pastel green (1231)
pastel blue (1232)
pastel skin colour (1234)

pintura:
cinnamon (1315)
perforating tools:
2-needle (11061)

embossing tools:
fine stylus (11031)
small ball (11011)

perga colors
exclusive (1431)

pattern: page 42

# Pastel blue card

## GENERAL

The outer card is made of ordinary parchment paper and the inner card is made of fantasy parchment ice blue.

## TRACING

White pencil: fold line. T gold: entire pattern, except flowers and leaves.

## PAINTING

T pastel blue: flowers. T pastel green: leaves. T pastel skin colour: flower hearts. PCE3, pintura cinnamon: dots in flower hearts.

## PERFORATING (SHALLOW)

With perforating tool 2-needle: according to pattern.

## EMBOSSING

With embossing tool fine stylus: fold line. With embossing tool small ball: between outlines of ornaments, flowers and leaves.

## PERFORATING (DEEP)

With perforating tool 2-needle: a second time according to pattern.

## CUTTING

Cut 2-needle perforations out between ornaments.

## FINISHING

Perforate with the 2-needle tool along arc in fold line. Cut these perforations open. Fold the card. Attach an oversized extra inner card made of fantasy parchment ice blue inside the outer card with removable tape. Perforate with perforating tool 2-needle along the card outline (through 4 layers). Cut the inner card and outer card out along these perforations. Attach the inner card in the outer card with double-sided tape.

## YOU WILL NEED

parchment paper:
parchment paper (1406)
fantasy parchment
red (1598)
fantasy parchment
lime green (1600)

tinta:
gold (1210)
red (1203)
yellow (1204)
leaf green (1213)
sepia (1207)

pintura:
white (1301)
yellow (1303)
bordeaux (1314)

perforating tools:
2-needle (11061)
4-needle (11051)
semi-star (1117)

embossing tools:
fine stylus (11031)
small ball (11011)
star (1122)

pattern: page 38

### GENERAL
The outer card is made of ordinary parchment paper and the inner card is made of fantasy parchment red. A piece of fantasy parchment lime green is attached behind the top star. 3-D elements: 2x parts of bow, made of ordinary parchment paper.

### TRACING
White pencil: fold line. T gold: outline card, outline of stars, lines around flame, lines on candle, lines on pine branches, 3-D elements. T red: outline of candle. T yellow: top part of candle and flame. T leaf green: lines on pine branches. T sepia: lines on pine branches.

### PAINTING
P white and P yellow mixed: top part of candle. P yellow + P bordeaux: flame.

### PERFORATING (SHALLOW)
With perforating tools 4-needle and semi-star: according to pattern.

### EMBOSSING
With embossing tool fine stylus: fold line. With embossing tool small ball: between outlines card and stars, dots on 4-needle perforations, candle, flame. With embossing tool star: according to pattern.

### PERFORATING (DEEP)
With perforating tools 4-needle and semi-star: a second time according to pattern.

### CUTTING
Cut 4-needle perforations into crosses.

### FINISHING
Cut a piece of fantasy parchment lime green to size and attach it with perga glue behind the front sheet of the card behind the star holding the candle. Attach an oversized extra inner card made of fantasy parchment red inside the outer card with removable tape. Perforate with perforating tool 2-needle along the card outline (through 4 layers). Cut the inner card and outer card out along these perforations. Attach the inner card in the outer card with double-sided tape.

## YOU WILL NEED

parchment paper:
parchment paper (1406)
fantasy parchment
apricot orange (1594)

tinta:
gold (1210)
leaf green (1213)

dorso nature colors (1444).
colour light green

pintura:
yellow (1303)
orange (1313)
brown (1307)
bordeaux (1314)
red (1302)
green (1305)

perforating tools:
2-needle (11061)
five in circle (1123)

embossing tools:
fine stylus (11031)
small ball (11011)

pattern: page 40

### GENERAL
The outer card is made of ordinary parchment paper and the inner card is made of fantasy parchment apricot orange.

### TRACING
White pencil: fold line. T gold: entire pattern, except flowers. T leaf green: stems and flowers in bud.

### PAINTING
P yellow: flower hearts. P orange: flowers. P brown and P bordeaux and P red mixed together: lines in flowers and dots in flower hearts. P yellow and green mixed: stems.

### DORSING WITH DORSO OIL
With dorso light green: behind flowers.

### PERFORATING (SHALLOW)
With perforating tool five in circle: according to pattern.

### EMBOSSING
With embossing tool fine stylus: fold line. With embossing tool small ball: dots in five in circle perforations, between gold lines, flowers (lightly).

### PERFORATING (DEEP)
With perforating tool five in circle: a second time according to pattern.

### FINISHING
Attach an oversized extra inner card made of fantasy parchment apricot orange inside the outer card with removable tape. Perforate with perforating tool 2-needle along the card outline (through 4 layers). Cut the inner card and outer card out along these perforations. Attach the inner card in the outer card with double-sided tape. Attach a piece of white paper, cut to size, on the front sheet of the inner card to find exactly behind the flowers.

## YOU WILL NEED

parchment paper:
parchment paper (1406)
fantasy parchment
hyacinth pink (1605)

tinta:
gold (1210)
pastel pink (1233)

perforating tools:
1-needle (11041)
2-needle (11061)
4-needle (11051)

embossing tools:
fine stylus (11031)
small ball (11011)

perga colors exclusive (1431)

pattern: page 40

# Cutaway card

### GENERAL
The outer card is made of ordinary parchment paper and the inner card is made of fantasy parchment hyacinth pink.

### TRACING
White pencil: fold line. T gold: entire pattern, except the leaves.

### PAINTING
T pastel pink + dab of PCE9: leaves.

### PERFORATING (SHALLOW)
With perforating tool 4-needle: according to pattern.

### EMBOSSING
With embossing tool fine stylus: fold line. With embossing tool small ball: dots between 4-needle perforations, between gold lines, dots between leaves.

### STIPPLING
With 1-needle tool: dots between leaves

### PERFORATING (DEEP)
With perforating tool 4-needle: a second time according to pattern. With perforating tool 2-needle: in four corners between card outline and decorative designs.

### CUTTING
Cut 2-needle perforations out in four corners between card outline and decorative designs. Cut 4-needle perforations into crosses.

### FINISHING
Attach an over-sized extra inner card made of fantasy parchment hyacinth pink inside the outer card with removable tape. Perforate with perforating tool 2-needle along the card outline (through 4 layers) and along the corner in the fold line. Cut the inner card and outer card out along these perforations. Attach the inner card in the outer card with double-sided tape.

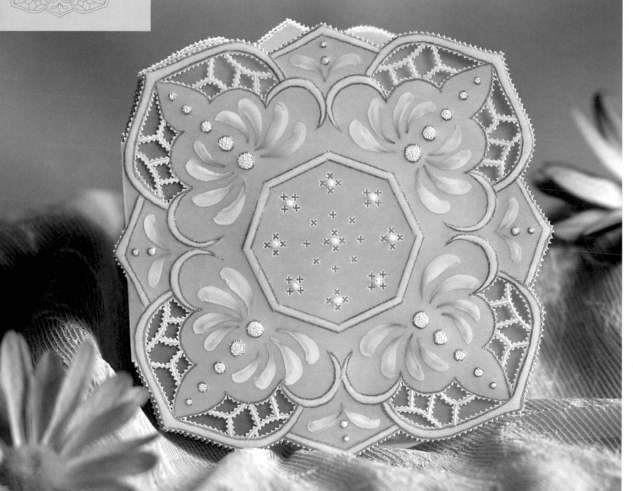

## YOU WILL NEED

parchment paper:
parchment paper (1406)
parchment paper
rainbow pastel (1486)

tinta:
gold (1210)
pastel blue (1232)
pastel skin colour (1234)

perforating tools:
2-needle (11061)
4-needle (11051)

embossing tools:
fine stylus (11031)
small ball (11011)

perga colors
exclusive (1431)

pattern: page 43

# *Pastel-coloured bouquet*

### GENERAL
The card is made of ordinary parchment paper and the insert sheet is made of parchment paper rainbow pastel.

### TRACING
White pencil: fold line. T gold: card outline, central border.

### PAINTING
T pastel blue+ PCE13: five small flowers. T pastel skin colour + PCE2: three small flowers. T pastel skin colour + PCE9: two large open flowers. T pastel skin colour + PCE7: one flower.

### COLORING WITH PERGA COLORS EXCLUSIVE
On front: PCE16: leaves and stems. PCE3: flower hearts.

### PERFORATING (SHALLOW)
With perforating tool 4-needle: according to pattern.

### EMBOSSING
With embossing tool fine stylus: fold line, diamond design according to pattern. With embossing tool small ball: between gold lines, flowers and leaves.

### PERFORATING (DEEP)
With perforating tool 4-needle: a second time according to pattern.

### CUTTING
Cut 4-needle perforations into crosses.

### FINISHING
Perforate with the 2-needle tool along arcs in fold line. Cut these perforations open. Attach an oversized extra inner card made of fantasy parchment rainbow pastel inside the card with removable tape. Perforate with perforating tool 2-needle along the card outline (through 3 layers). Cut the card and the insert sheet out along these perforations. Attach the insert sheet in the card with double-sided tape. With T gold, place a few dots and lines in the flowers.

## YOU WILL NEED

parchment paper:
parchment paper (1406)
fantasy parchment
hyacinth pink (1605)

tinta:
white (1201)
leaf green (1213)
purple (1208)
sepia (1207)

pintura:
yellow (1303)
green (1305)
skin colour (1308):
yellow ochre (1312)

perforating tools:
2-needle (11061)
4-needle (11051)

embossing tools:
fine stylus (11031)
small ball (11011)

pattern: page 39

# *Lilac flowers*

### GENERAL
The outer card is made of ordinary parchment paper and the inner card is made of fantasy parchment hyacinth pink.

### TRACING
White pencil: fold line. T white: entire pattern, except painting in the middle. T leaf green: leaves and stems. T purple, thinned: flowers.

### PAINTING
P yellow + P green: leaves and stems. P skin colour + dab of T purple: flowers. P yellow ochre: flower hearts. T sepia: pistils.

### PERFORATING (SHALLOW)
With perforating tool 4-needle: according to pattern.

### EMBOSSING
With embossing tool fine stylus: fold line, diamond design according to pattern.
With embossing tool small ball: between outlines of card outline and central border, bottom of flowers.

### PERFORATING (DEEP)
With perforating tool 4-needle: a second time according to pattern.

### CUTTING
Cut 4-needle perforations into crosses.

### FINISHING
Perforate with the 2-needle tool along arcs in fold line. Cut these perforations open. Attach an oversized extra inner card made of fantasy parchment hyacinth pink inside the card with removable tape. Perforate with perforating tool 2-needle along the card outline (through 4 layers). Cut the outer card and inner card out along these perforations. Attach the inner card in the outer card with double-sided tape.

# Butterflies

### GENERAL
The outer card is made of ordinary parchment paper and the inner card is made of fantasy parchment apricot orange.

### TRACING
White pencil: fold line. T black: entire pattern.

### PAINTING WITH PERGA COLORS EXCLUSIVE
On front: PCE2: flowers. PCE3: highlights in flowers. PCE16 + PCE17: leaves and stems. PCE17: lines between semi-square perforations. PCE1: butterfly wings. PCE7: outside of butterfly wings. PCE19: middle of butterfly wings. PCE3: border on edge, border around butterflies.

### PERFORATING (SHALLOW)
With perforating tool semi-square: according to pattern.

### EMBOSSING
With embossing tool fine stylus: fold line. With embossing tool small ball: flowers, butterflies.

### PERFORATING (DEEP)
With perforating tool semi-square: a second time according to pattern.

### CUTTING
Cut out the central perforations of the semi-square perforations.

### FINISHING
Fold the card and perforate along the card outline with the 2-needle tool. Cut the card out along these perforations. Cut a piece of fantasy parchment lime green to size and attach it behind the border around butterflies with perga glue. Cut the inner card to size and attach it inside the card with double-sided tape.

## YOU WILL NEED

parchment paper:
parchment paper (1406)
fantasy parchment
red (1598)
fantasy parchment
ice blue (1590)

tinta:
white (1201)
gold (1210)
leaf green (1213)
red (1203)
sepia (1207)

pintura:
yellow (1303)
green (1305)
red (1302)
black (1311)
cinnamon (1315):
white (1301)

pinta perla:
bronze (1521)
yellow (1516)
white (1501)
green (1508)

perforating tools:
2-needle (11061)
corner (1130)

embossing tools:
fine stylus (11031)
small ball (11011)

pattern: page 46

# Winter scene

### GENERAL

The outer card is made of ordinary parchment paper and the inner card is made of fantasy parchment red. 3-D element: 1x roof of church made of ordinary parchment paper.

### TRACING

White pencil: fold line. T gold: card outline, ornaments in central border, outline of stars. T leaf green: holly leaves, parts of trees (see colour example). T red: berries. T sepia: church. T white: parts of trees (see colour example), lines in snow, 3-D roof of church.

### PAINTING

P yellow + P green + P perla bronze: holly leaves. P red: berries. P black: dot on berries. T white: shiny spot on berries. P cinnamon + P perla bronze: church. P perla yellow: windows of church. P white: 3-D roof of church. P perla white: snow. P green + P perla green: parts of trees. P white: parts of trees.

### PERFORATING (SHALLOW)

With perforating tool corner: according to pattern.

### EMBOSSING

With embossing tool fine stylus: fold line. With embossing tool small ball: squares in corner perforations, ornaments of central border, holly leaves, berries, trees, snow, 3-D roof of church.

### PERFORATING (DEEP)

With perforating tool corner: a second time according to pattern.

### FINISHING

Fold the outer card and perforate along the card outline with the 2-needle tool. Cut the card out along these perforations.

Cut a piece of fantasy parchment ice blue to size and attach it behind the central with perga glue. Cut the inner card to size and attach it inside the card with double-sided tape. Cut out the 3-D element and attach it to the card with a dabs of perga kit.

# Pastel flowers

## YOU WILL NEED

parchment paper:
parchment paper (1406)
fantasy parchment
lavender blue (1602)

tinta:
gold (1210)
pastel blue (1232)

pintura:
orange (1313)

perforating tools:
2-needle (11061)
5-needle (1112)

embossing tools:
fine stylus (11031)
extra fine ball (11071)
small ball (11011)

perga colors
exclusive (1431)

pattern: page 43

### GENERAL
The outer card is made of ordinary parchment paper and the inner card is made of fantasy parchment lavender blue.

### TRACING
White pencil: fold line. T gold: outline of inner card, outline of central border of outer card.

### PAINTING
T pastel blue+ PCE13: small flowers. T pastel blue+ PCE11: large flowers. PCE17: leaves. P orange: flower hearts.

### PERFORATING (SHALLOW)
With perforating tools 2-needle and 5-needle: according to pattern on front sheet of outer card.

### EMBOSSING
With embossing tool fine stylus: fold line. With embossing tool extra fine ball: circles around middle 5-needle perforations. With embossing tool small ball: between gold lines of central border, flowers and large leaves.

### PERFORATING (DEEP)
With perforating tools 2-needle and 5-needle (swivel tool to left and right): a second time according to pattern on front sheet of outer card.

### CUTTING
Cut out the 2-needle perforations in the central border.

### FINISHING
Cut the front sheet of the outer card out along the 5-needle perforations and trim the back sheet straight. Fold the inner card and perforate along the card outline with the 2-needle tool. Cut the inner card out along these perforations. Attach the inner card in the outer card with double-sided tape.

**YOU WILL NEED**

parchment paper:
parchment paper (1406)
fantasy parchment
bordeaux (1588)

tinta:
gold (1210)
white (1201)

perforating tools:
2-needle (11061)
4-needle (11051)
semi-circle (1109)
five in circle (1123)

embossing tools:
fine stylus (11031)
extra fine ball (11071)
small ball (11011)

pattern: page 44

## GENERAL
The outer card is made of ordinary parchment paper and the inner card is made of fantasy parchment bordeaux.

## TRACING
White pencil: fold line. T gold: card outline, leaves and stems, lines at semi-circle perforations. T white: flowers.

## PERFORATING (SHALLOW)
With perforating tools 4-needle tool, semi-circle and five in circle: according to pattern.

## EMBOSSING
With embossing tool fine stylus: fold line. With embossing tool extra fine ball: dots between five in circle and 4-needle perforations, semi-circles between semi-circle perforations, along gold line in card outline. With embossing tool small ball: flowers and leaves.

## PERFORATING (DEEP)
With perforating tools 4-needle tool, semi-circle and five in circle: a second time according to pattern.

## CUTTING
Cut 4-needle perforations into crosses.

## FINISHING
Attach an oversized extra inner card made of fantasy parchment bordeaux inside the card with removable tape. Perforate with perforating tool 2-needle along the card outline (through 4 layers). Cut the outer card and inner card out along these perforations. Attach the inner card in the outer card with double-sided tape.

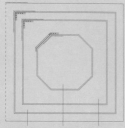

## YOU WILL NEED

parchment paper:
fantasy parchment
ime green (1600)
fantasy parchment
moss green (1601)
parchment vellum
winter birds (2517)

tinta:
pastel green (1231)

perforating tools:
2-needle (11061)
4-needle (11051)

embossing tools:
extra fine ball (11071)

pattern: page 48

# Winter birds

*The following are general instructions for both pieces and card. If a certain piece of text is specifically for one of the three objects, then this is indicated.*

### CARD, GENERAL

The card is made of fantasy parchment moss green. Three extra front sheets are attached to the front sheet. The first extra front sheet is made of fantasy parchment lime green, the second of parchment vellum winter birds and the third of fantasy parchment moss green.

### LARGE PIECES, GENERAL

The pieces are made of fantasy parchment moss green/fantasy parchment lime green. Three times four extra front sheets are attached to the front sheet. The first four extra front sheets are made of fantasy parchment lime green/fantasy parchment

moss green, the second four extra front sheets are made of parchment vellum winter birds and the third four extra front sheets are made of fantasy parchment moss green/fantasy parchment lime green.

### TRACING

White pencil: fold line. T pastel green: outlines on card and 1st and 3rd extra front sheets.

### PERFORATING (DEEP)

With perforating tool 4-needle: according to pattern on 1st and 3rd extra front sheet(s). With perforating tool 2-needle: passe partout on 3rd extra front sheet(s).

pattern: page 47

# Winter birds

## CUTTING
Cut out the 2-needle perforations in the passe partout.

## CARD, FINISHING
Fold the card. Perforate with the 2-needle tool along the outline of the card and the extra front sheets. Cut the card and the extra front sheets out along these perforations. Place a drop of tinta pastel green on the tear-off palette pad. Dip the embossing tool extra fine ball in this and use it to place small dots between the 4-needle perforations. Attach a piece of white paper, cut to size, behind the 1st and 3rd extra front sheet with perga spray. Attach the 1st extra front sheet to the front sheet of the card with perga glue. Cut out a bird of your choice from the parchment vellum winter birds and cut it to size. Attach it to white paper and attach this on the first extra front sheet. Attach the 3rd extra front sheet to the 2nd extra front sheet.

# Winter birds

### FINISHING PIECES

Cut the piece out along the outline. Attach a piece of fantasy parchment lime green/fantasy parchment moss green behind this. Perforate with the 2-needle tool along the outline of the extra front sheets. Cut the extra front sheets out along these perforations. Place a drop of tinta pastel green on the tear-off palette pad.
Dip the embossing tool extra fine ball in this and use it to place small dots between the 4-needle perforations.
Attach a piece of white paper, cut to size, behind the 1st and 3rd extra front sheets with perga spray.
Attach the first four extra front sheets to the front sheet of the card with perga glue. Cut out a bird of your choice from the parchment vellum winter birds and cut it to size. Attach it to white paper and attach this on the first extra front sheet. Attach the 3rd extra front sheets to the 2nd extra front sheets.

# Fan

### GENERAL
The fan is made of ordinary parchment paper and consists of nine parts. 3-D element: 9x butterfly made of ordinary parchment paper. Repeat the following steps nine times.

### TRACING
T white: entire pattern.

### PERFORATING (SHALLOW)
With perforating tool 5-needle. according to pattern.

### EMBOSSING
With embossing tool extra fine ball: circles around middle 5-needle perforations, lines around 5-needle perforations, lines in butterfly wings on fan, body of butterfly of 3-D element. With embossing tool hockey stick: ornaments.

### EMBOSSING ON GRID
With embossing tool small ball: in top part of fan, borders A according to pattern A.

### PERFORATING (DEEP)
With perforating tool 5-needle: a second time according to pattern (swivel to left and right): With perforating tool 2-needle: top part of fan according to pattern, butterfly wings of 3-D element.

### CUTTING
Cut out 2-needle perforations in top part of fan and 3-D element according to pattern.

### FINISHING
Perforate with perforating tool 2-needle along the outline of the fan, cut the fan out along these perforations. Attach the butterfly to the fan part with perga glue. Attach a small silver paste jewel to the 3-D element, as the eye of the butterfly.

1x

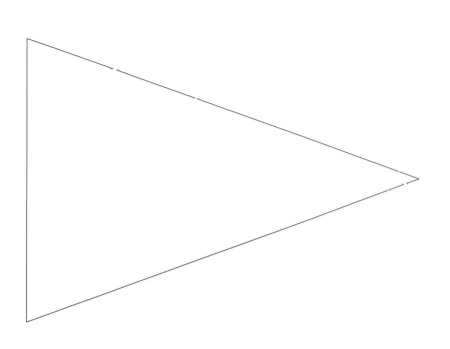

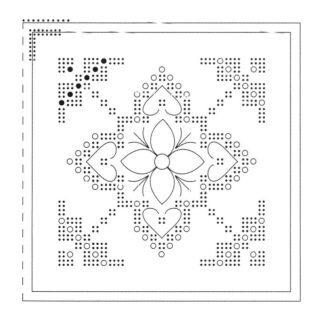

1x

4x

**FLOWER BEADS**

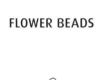

21x

# CHRISTMAS ROSE IN STAR

A

embossing / cutting

A

## HEART CARD

A

A

A

A

A

A

embossing / cutting

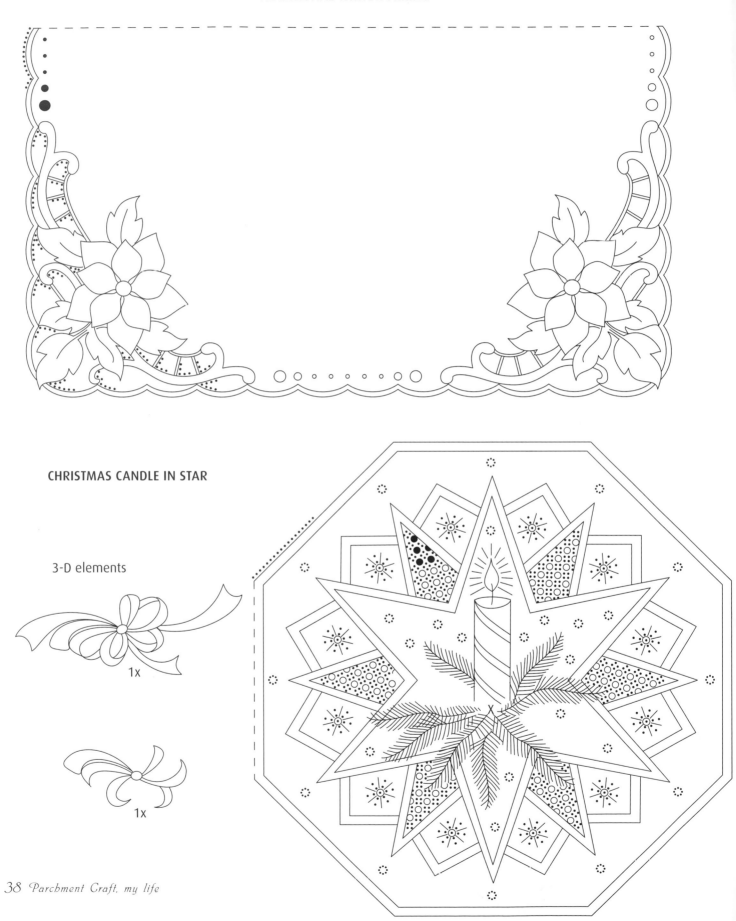

**CHRISTMAS CANDLE IN STAR**

3-D elements

1x

1x

**NATURAL INTERWEAVING**

**LILAC FLOWERS**

**CUTAWAY CARD**

**ORANGE FLOWER SET**

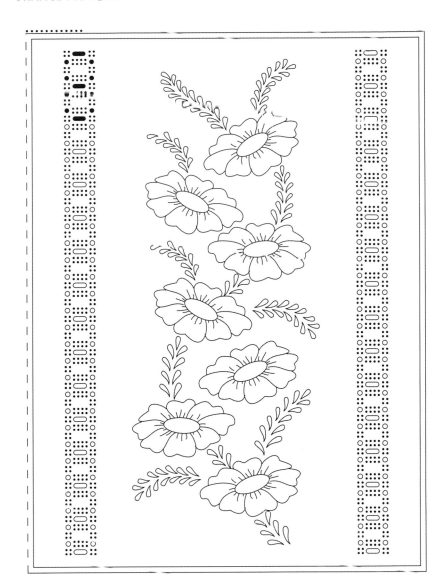

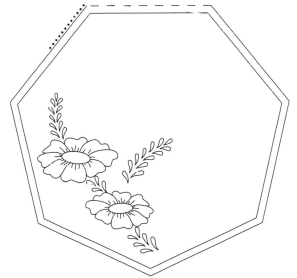

**PASTEL BLUE CARD**

**PASTEL-COLOURED BOUQUET**

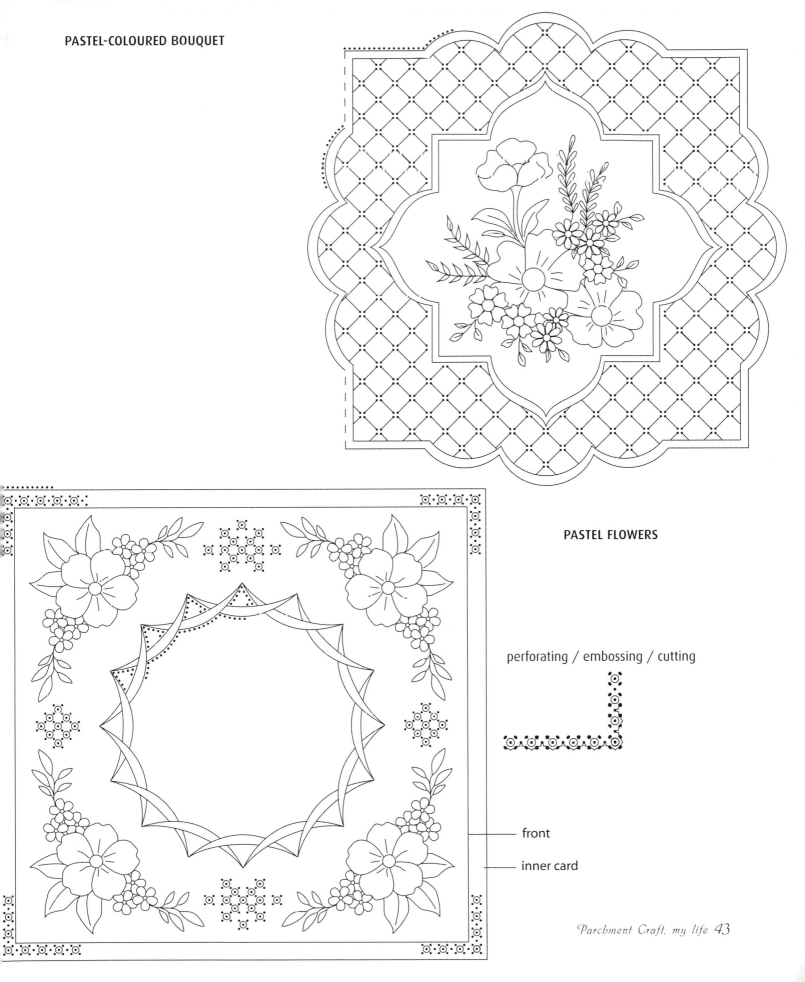

**PASTEL FLOWERS**

perforating / embossing / cutting

front

inner card

ELEGANT WHITEWORKING

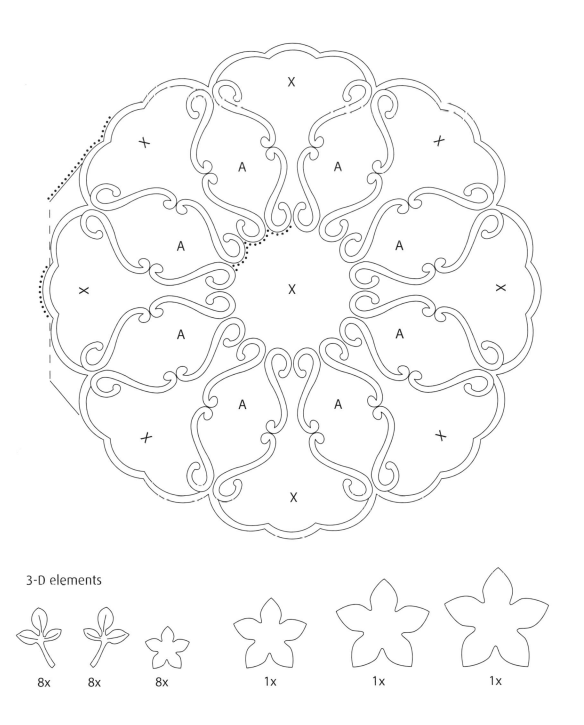

3-D elements

8x     8x     8x     1x     1x     1x

embossing / cutting

A

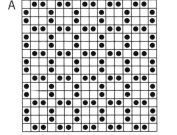 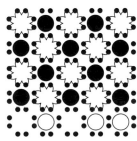

3-D element

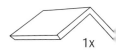

1x

**BUTTERFLIES**

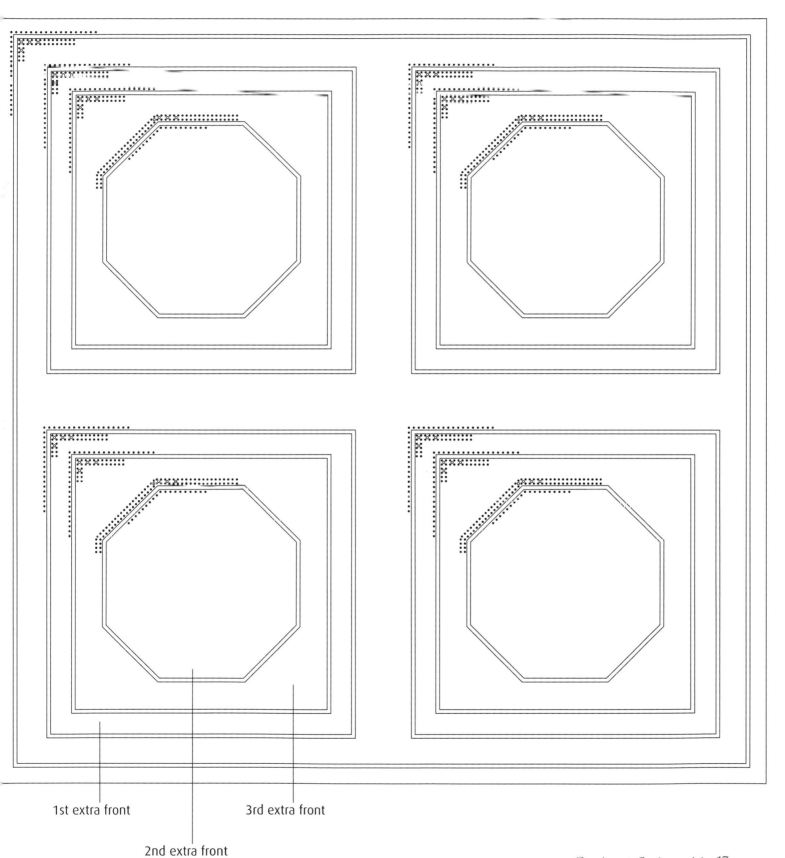

1st extra front

2nd extra front

3rd extra front

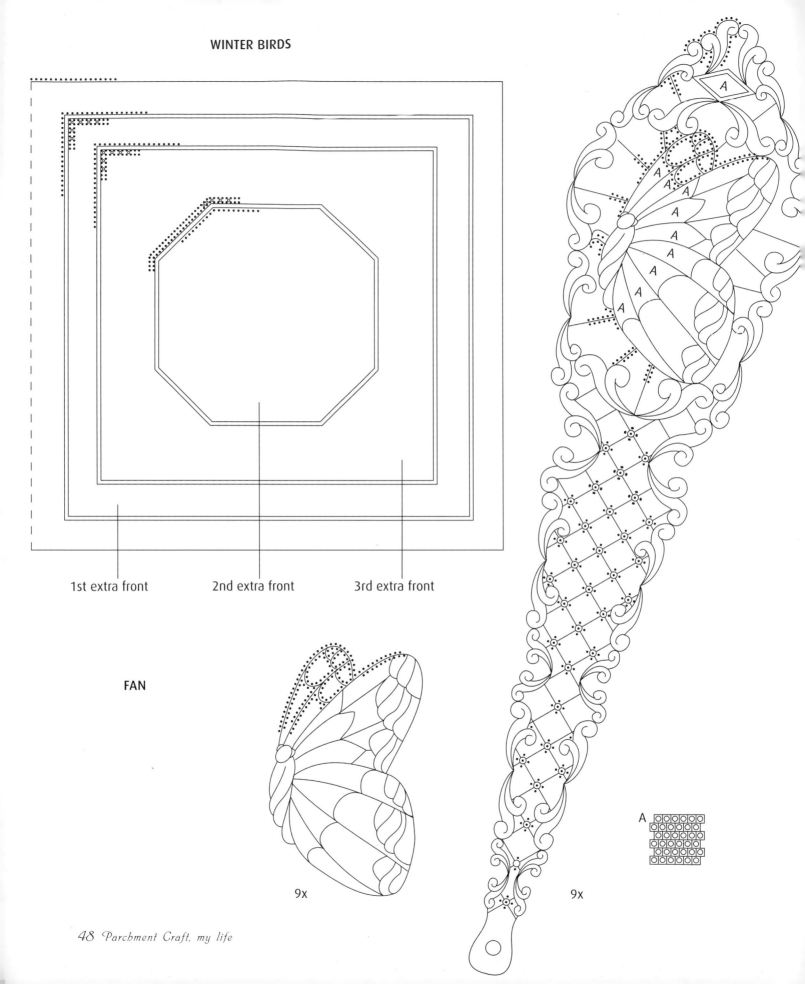

**WINTER BIRDS**

1st extra front        2nd extra front        3rd extra front

**FAN**

9x

9x

A